T0288629

Frankenstein

LEVEL ONE   400 HEADWORDS

OXFORD
UNIVERSITY PRESS

Great Clarendon Street, Oxford, OX2 6DP, United Kingdom

Oxford University Press is a department of the University of Oxford.
It furthers the University's objective of excellence in research, scholarship,
and education by publishing worldwide. Oxford is a registered trade
mark of Oxford University Press in the UK and in certain other countries

© Oxford University Press 2013

The moral rights of the author have been asserted

First published in Dominoes 2013

2023

20

ISBN: 978 0 19 424977 5   BOOK
ISBN: 978 0 19 463937 8   BOOK AND AUDIO PACK

Printed in China

This book is printed on paper from certified and well-managed sources

ACKNOWLEDGEMENTS

Cover image: Getty Images (Toward the light/Massimo Merlini/Vetta)

Illustrations by: Fabio Leone/Bright Agency

The publisher would like to thank the following for kind permission to reproduce photographs: Alamy
Images pp.42 (Mary Wollstonecraft Shelley/Lebrecht Music and Arts Photo Library),
43 (Gaston Leroux/Mary Evans Picture Library); Corbis p.38 (Ice cap in the Disco Bay/Patrick
Robert); Getty Images pp.18 (Ski slopes/Andreas Voegele Photo), 24 (Snow-capped forest/
PhotoAlto/Jerome Gorin); Kobal Collection pp.43 (The Phantom of the Opera, 2004/Really
Useful Films/Joel Schumacher Prods.), 44 (Dr Jekyll and Mr Hyde, 1941/MGM), 44 (Dorian
Gray, 2009/Ealing Studios), 44 (The Mummy Returns, 2001/Alphaville/Imhotep Prod); Mary
Evans Picture Library p.6 (Geneva across the lake, circa 1840/Engraving by J Schoeder);
Oxford University Press p.7 (Lightning/Photodisc).

DOMINOES

Series Editors: Bill Bowler and Sue Parminter

Frankenstein

Mary Shelley

Text adaptation by Bill Bowler

Illustrated by Fabio Leone

Mary Shelley (1797–1851) was the second wife of the English Romantic poet Percy Bysshe Shelley. In 1816 the Shelleys spent the summer in Geneva with the English poet Lord Byron, Dr John Polidori, and Mary's stepsister and Byron's lover – Claire Clairmont. One cold, rainy day, they began to tell ghost stories round the fire. Byron had the idea of everyone writing a horror story, and Mary wrote *Frankenstein* as a result. It was published in 1818. Mary later wrote a number of other novels and short stories, but *Frankenstein* remains her most famous book.

OXFORD
UNIVERSITY PRESS

BEFORE READING

1 Here are some of the characters in *Frankenstein*. Match each sentence with a number in the picture below.

a Alphonse Frankenstein, Victor's father. ☐

b Caroline Frankenstein, Victor's mother. ☐

c Victor Frankenstein, the monster maker. ☐

d Elizabeth Lavenza. She lives with the Frankensteins. Victor calls her 'cousin'. ☐

e Ernest, Victor's younger brother. ☐

f William, Victor's youngest brother. ☐

g Henry Clerval, Victor's best friend. ☐

2 At university, Victor makes a monster. But soon it begins killing his family and friends. Answer these questions.

a Who does the monster kill, do you think? Why?

b What do you think happens to Victor in the end?

c What do you think happens to the monster?

CHAPTER 1

ON A SHIP IN THE ICE

*On a **ship** in the cold Arctic **ice**, Robert Walton's new friend began to tell the story of his **life**.*

My name is Victor Frankenstein. My father, Alphonse, came from Geneva. He met my mother when his best friend, Beaufort, died. Beaufort left his daughter, Caroline, with no money. Where could she live? My father found her a room in his **cousin** Louisa's house. Two years later, he **married** her.

After they married, my father took her to Germany, France, and Italy. I was born in Naples, and for some time I was their only child.

One day, when I was about five, my father was away in Milan. My mother and I visited **Lake** Como. Near the lake, we saw the house of a **poor** family. The man and his wife had five children. Four of these had dark hair and eyes. The fifth – a quiet young girl – had beautiful yellow hair and blue eyes. My mother always wanted a daughter, and was interested in this little girl.

ship you use a ship to go across the water

ice water that is hard when it is very cold

life (*plural* **lives**) you live this

cousin the son (or daughter) of your father's (or mother's) brother (or sister)

marry to make someone your husband or wife

lake a lot of water with land around it

poor without much money; something you say when you feel sorry for someone

When my mother spoke to the poor woman, she told her the girl's story. Elizabeth Lavenza (that was the girl's name) was the daughter of a German woman and a Milanese man from a good family. When she was born, her mother died. So her father left her with the family by the lake. The poor woman gave the child a bed, milk, and love, and the girl's father gave her money for that. But then the Austrians took him and put him in **prison**, and he died there. Now the girl had no family and no money, and things were far from easy for the poor family.

My mother felt sorry and spoke to the woman. After that, Elizabeth came and lived in our house. I played with her and called her 'cousin'. I was a year older than her, and she was more than a sister to me.

After my younger brother Ernest was born, my mother and father took us all to Switzerland. We had a town house in Geneva, but lived mostly in a country house in Belrive, by the lake. I went to school and made friends with one of the schoolboys. His name was Henry Clerval and his father had a shop in Geneva. I was a happy child. This was before my life changed, before things went wrong.

When I was about thirteen, I found – and began reading – a book by the old **alchemist** Cornelius Agrippa.

'There are many better writers,' my father laughed.

But I found the book interesting. And when I finished it, I read books by different alchemists. 'Perhaps one day I can stop **death**, and people can live for hundreds of years,' I thought. 'Then I can be rich and famous.'

My youngest brother William was born about that time.

When I was fifteen, I remember a big **storm** on the lake one night. I saw the white **lightning** in the dark sky. And

prison a place where people must stay when they do something wrong

alchemist someone who thinks that they can change cheap things into gold, and stay alive for hundreds of years

death the time when someone or something dies

storm lots of rain and bad weather

lightning the light in the sky when there is a storm

then, suddenly, some lightning hit a big old tree by the lake and broke it in two. A famous **science** teacher was at our house in Belrive at the time, and he told me all about lightning. Suddenly the science of today was more interesting for me than books by dead alchemists.

When I was seventeen, I finished school in Geneva and my father told me, 'Now you must go and learn at the **University** of Ingolstadt.'

Before I could leave, Elizabeth was suddenly ill with a **fever**. She nearly died. But my mother sat by her bed and **looked after** her.

After three days, Elizabeth was well again and could get out of bed. But my mother now had the fever badly. She called Elizabeth and me to her, and spoke quietly to us.

'Victor, I'm dying,' she said, 'Please marry Elizabeth. I wanted to see that happy day, but my husband must see it now. And Elizabeth, please look after my young children. Now I must leave you. Perhaps we can meet again in the life after death.'

science the study of the natural world

university people study here after they finish school

fever when you get very hot because you are ill

look after to do things for someone or something that needs help

3

Soon after that, she died. I left Elizabeth, my father, and my brothers in Geneva and went to Ingolstadt.

Henry Clerval wanted to go to university there, too. But his father said 'no'. Work was more important than university for Henry's father.

So I began my student life without Henry. I took cheap rooms in an old house in town when I arrived. Next day, I met two important university teachers – **Monsieur** Krempe and Monsieur Waldman. Monsieur Krempe laughed at my talk of alchemists. I didn't like him. Monsieur Waldman didn't laugh, and I liked him a lot. Through him, I began to be very interested in science.

I looked carefully at lots of dead bodies. What makes life? What brings death? In the end, I found the answers to these two important questions. After that, in my rooms in town I began to make a **creature** from **parts** of dead bodies. I worked day and night. My face was now white, and I was ill. I forgot my family, my friends, and my teachers for months.

One November night, when there was a storm in the sky, I finished. The creature on the table before me was suddenly alive. He opened one big, yellow eye and looked up at me. 'Ugh!' I cried. I felt afraid, and ran from the room.

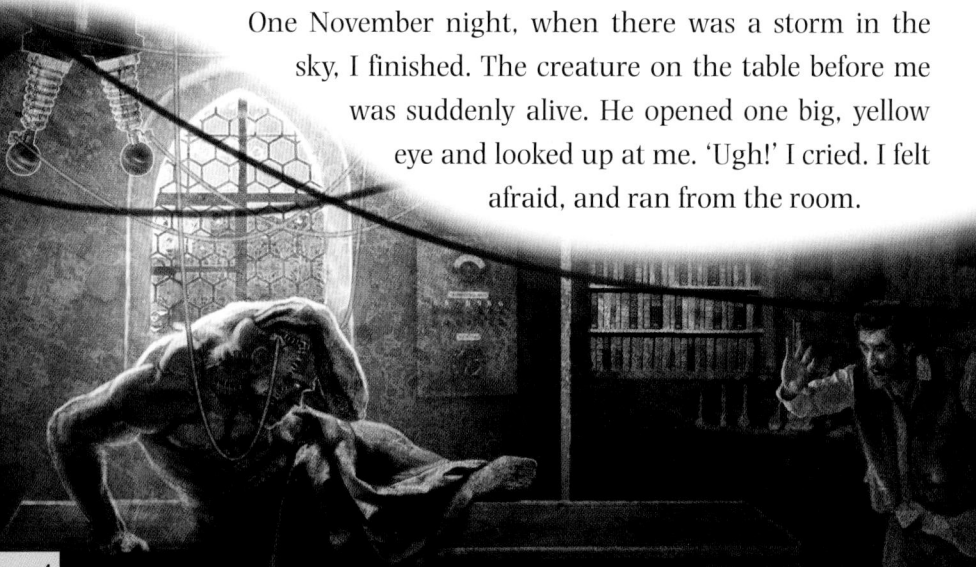

After some hours, I met Henry Clerval in the street.

'What are you doing here, my friend?' I asked him.

'I arrived this morning. I'm a university student,' he answered. 'My father said 'yes' in the end. But what's the matter? Are you ill?'

'I'm tired from work,' I said.

'Then let's go to your rooms at once,' said Henry.

'Is the creature waiting there?' I thought. But there was no creature when we arrived.

I went to bed at once. I had a fever. Henry stayed and looked after me for months. When I was well again, Henry put a letter from Elizabeth into my hands. I read it with interest.

Cousin Victor,

Henry tells us all about you. You're well now, and I'm happy for that! Here, your brother Ernest is now fifteen and little William is five. Your father is well and we have a new person in the house – Justine Moritz. Her family is dead and she now lives with us. She's a nice young woman and a good **servant**, too.

Please write soon.

Elizabeth Lavenza

servant a person who works for someone rich

READING CHECK

Choose the best words to complete each sentence.

a Victor tells Robert Walton his story in the *Arctic* / *Antarctic*.

b Victor's father, Alphonse, came from *Paris* / *Geneva*.

c Alphonse married his best friend's *sister* / *daughter*, Caroline.

d Victor was born in *Naples* / *Milan*.

e Caroline took a poor *girl* / *woman* into her family in Italy.

f Elizabeth Lavenza's father died *at sea* / *in prison*.

g Victor had *two* / *three* young brothers.

h Henry Clerval was Victor's best friend at *work* / *school*.

i When Victor was seventeen, his mother *died* / *ran away*.

j Victor was a science student at *Ingolstadt* / *Milan* University.

k When his creature came alive, Victor felt *afraid* / *excited*.

l Victor ran from his rooms, but the monster *stayed* / *died*.

m After Clerval arrived, Victor was ill for *days* / *months*.

n Later, he read *his father's* / *Elizabeth's* nice letter from home.

o It spoke of Justine Moritz, the Frankensteins' *new* / *old* servant.

ACTIVITIES

WORD WORK

Use a set of three words in the sky to complete each sentence.

life / ice / ship

alchemists / university / monsieur

marry/ cousin / death

fever / poor / looked after

storm / lightning / lake

creature / science / parts

a On a ......ship...... in the ....ice......., Victor tells the story of his ......life...... .

b At fifteen, Victor saw a .... with ....on ....Geneva.

c When ....Elizabeth was ill with a very bad ...., Mrs Frankenstein .... her.

d Did Victor ....his ....Elizabeth after his mother's ....?

e At Ingolstadt ...., ... Krempe laughed at Victor because he found ....interesting.

f Because he was interested in ...., Victor made a ....from dead body ....

GUESS WHAT

What happens in the next chapter? Tick five boxes.

a Victor stops being a science student at Ingolstadt. ☐

b Victor marries Elizabeth. ☐

c One of Victor's brothers dies. ☐

d Victor sees his creature near Geneva. ☐

e Victor tells his family about the creature. ☐

f The creature kills Victor's father. ☐

g Justine Moritz goes to prison. ☐

h Justine Moritz dies. ☐

i Victor kills the creature. ☐

7

CHAPTER 2
WILLIAM AND JUSTINE

I took Henry to the university the next day. It wasn't easy. When I met my teachers, Monsieur Krempe and Monsieur Waldman, I didn't feel good. And when they talked of science, I felt very ill. Because Henry was a student of languages, I **decided** to change to languages, too. After that, I felt a lot better.

So Henry and I learnt languages at the university. I wanted to go home to Geneva in the last days of the autumn. But the weather that year was bad, with lots of **snow** and cold nights. So in the end I stayed in Ingolstadt for the winter. With the new year, I began to think again of visiting my family. But before I left for Geneva in the spring, Henry and I went for a week to the **mountains** near Ingolstadt. The mountain walks were good for me. I loved the green country, the blue skies, the warm sun, and the beautiful spring flowers.

But when we came back to Ingolstadt, there was a letter for me from my father. I read it quickly, and felt afraid once more.

decide to think of something and then do it

snow something soft, cold, and white

mountain a big hill

news when someone tells you something that is new

Plainpalais /ˌplæɲpæˈle/

locket a little, flat, expensive box that you wear round your neck, usually with a picture of someone that you love in it

Victor, my son,

I have some very bad **news** for you. Your brother William is dead! Yesterday evening, he and Ernest went walking in the open country at **Plainpalais**. William ran away, and Ernest couldn't find him. We looked for him all night. Then at five this morning, I found him – dead under a tree. Someone killed him, and took his **locket** with the picture of your mother in it.

Come home soon, dear son. Elizabeth, Ernest, and I need you here.

With love, your father,

Alphonse Frankenstein

8

I left for Geneva at once. But when I arrived, it was dark and the town **gates** were not open. So I took a **boat** across the lake to Plainpalais.

There was a very bad storm that night with lots of rain and lightning.

'William, this storm is for you, my brother. The weather's angry about your death!' I cried.

And then I saw something under some trees in front of me. It was my creature – the **monster** from my student rooms in Ingolstadt.

'What's he doing here?' I thought. And then I suddenly understood. 'He's my young brother's killer!' I said. He was, I knew it. I could feel it.

Just then, the monster moved quickly past me and ran away to the hills. When they opened the town gates in the morning, I went to my family home and to bed.

gate a big door into, or out of, a town

boat you go across water in this; a little ship

monster a person that is very bad to look at, or does very bad things

When I got up, my brother Ernest had more news.

'They've got William's killer,' he said.

'What? But how? When did they catch him?'

'Not *him*, Victor – *her*. It's Justine Moritz. A servant found William's locket in her pocket the day after he died. She's in prison now.'

Just then, my father arrived.

'Justine isn't the killer!' I cried.

'Ah, Elizabeth too thinks differently,' my father said. 'But then who killed William?'

I couldn't tell my family about the monster. How could I talk about bringing life to a dead body? It was a **mad** story, and I didn't want to finish my life in a hospital for mad people. So I said nothing.

That afternoon, Elizabeth and I visited Justine in prison.

'You aren't William's killer,' Elizabeth said to her. 'Victor and I know that.'

But the next day, **lawyers** began questioning Justine.

'Where were you on the night of William Frankenstein's death?' one of them asked.

'That evening I visited a cousin in a village not far from Geneva,' Justine answered. 'When I came back to the town, I heard about William. I went and looked for him for hours, but found nothing. Then, because the town gates weren't open, I went and sat under a tree. Perhaps I slept for some minutes there, but then someone came near me. So I got up.'

'Why was the locket in your coat pocket?' the lawyer asked.

'Perhaps the killer put it there,' Justine said. 'But why? And when? I'm sorry, but I don't know.'

There were more questions and more answers.

mad about things that people could think are not true; thinking things that are not true

lawyer someone who questions people when they do something wrong

Elizabeth spoke for Justine. 'She's a good young woman – a servant in our house, not a killer.'

I said nothing.

In the end, I could listen no more. I went home and slept very badly that night.

The next day, Justine told the lawyers, 'You can stop questioning me. I was the boy's killer.'

Then the **judge** spoke.

'Justine Moritz must die for this,' he said.

That evening, Elizabeth and I visited Justine again.

'Justine, you're not William's killer. Why did you say that earlier today?' cried Elizabeth.

'I'm sorry,' answered Justine. 'You're right. I didn't kill William. But the **priest** visited me many times and said, "You killed this boy, you monster! Speak truly now!" In the end, I was tired. So I answered "yes".'

Early the next morning, Justine was dead.

Soon after that, we went to our country house in Belrive. I went for long walks. I often took a boat out on the lake. I wanted to forget the past months. 'Why am I here when William and Justine are dead?' I thought. 'They did nothing wrong, and I killed them. Perhaps I can find death in the cold waters of the lake.' But I stayed alive for Elizabeth, for my father, and for Ernest.

judge a person who says when something is right or wrong

priest a man who works for the church

ACTIVITIES

READING CHECK

Complete the sentences with the correct names.

Alphonse

Elizabeth

Henry

Justine

The monster

Victor

William

a ..... Victor ..... begins to learn languages with ....

b .... and .... go walking in the mountains near Ingolstadt.

c .... writes a letter from Geneva about .... 's death.

d .... goes to Geneva and sees .... at Plainpalais.

e 'He's .... 's killer,' thinks ....

f .... runs to the hills, and .... goes to his family home.

g .... is in prison, ... learns the next morning.

h The day after .... died, they found his locket in .... 's pocket.

i .... says nothing about .... to his family.

j .... and .... visit the prison that afternoon.

k .... speaks for .... when the lawyers ask questions.

l 'I was .... 's killer!' .... tells the lawyers.

m .... says nothing, and so .... dies.

12

WORD WORK

Find words in the lockets to complete the sentences.

a Victor ...~~decides~~... to stop learning science at University.

b The .... is bad that winter, so he stays in Ingolstadt.

c He can't go into Geneva before the town .... open.

d He takes a .... across the lake to Plainpalais.

e He sees the .... there, but tells nobody about it.

f He doesn't want to be in a hospital for .... people.

g Ernest tells Victor the latest .... the next morning.

h The .... ask Justine about the locket in her pocket.

i The .... visits Justine many times and says, 'Speak truly!'

j The .... says, 'Justine Moritz must die.'

cedised

wons

stega

toba

rotsnem

dam

wens

reyswa

tsirep

dugej

GUESS WHAT

What happens in the next chapter? Tick a box for 1 and a box for 2.

1 Victor ...
- **a** ☐ goes back to university.
- **b** ☐ tells Elizabeth about the monster.
- **c** ☐ tells his father about the monster.
- **d** ☐ meets the monster in the mountains.

2 The monster ...
- **a** ☐ kills Henry Clerval in Ingolstadt.
- **b** ☐ talks about its life and William's death.
- **c** ☐ takes Elizabeth away to the mountains.
- **d** ☐ kills Ernest in his bed.

CHAPTER 3
THE MONSTER'S STORY

I needed to do something different. So I decided to visit the mountains near my home. Perhaps there I could forget **sad** things and feel better. First, I went on my horse up to the village of **Chamonix**. I saw cold mountain rivers, snow on dark trees, and tall, white mountains in front of me. It was beautiful and I felt very happy. But the next day it rained and I felt sad once more. How could I change that? 'I know! I can go up **Montanvert**!' I cried. 'I can look down on everything from there.'

So next morning, I began walking. At twelve o'clock, I was far up the mountain. There was a **glacier** between it and the next mountain. I walked across. Then I sat down and looked back at Montanvert and **Mont Blanc** behind it.

Suddenly, I saw a man on the glacier. He was very big and he moved very fast on his feet. I watched him carefully. When he came nearer, I could see him better. It was my creature! I felt ill.

'Go away!' I cried. 'I don't want to see you near me or my family again, you monster.'

'Why do you **hate** me?' he asked. 'You made me.'

'What do you want from me?'

'I want to tell you the story of my life. Please listen.'

'Never!' I cried.

'Then I must kill more of your family. Do you want that?'

'No,' I answered. 'Tell me your story. I'm listening.'

'Not here,' the creature said. 'Come with me across the glacier. My **hut**, with a warm **fire** in it, isn't far. You can listen to me there.'

sad not happy

Chamonix
/ˈʃæmɒnɪ/

Montanvert
/mɒntænˈveə/

glacier a cold river of ice that moves very slowly

Mont Blanc
/ˌmɒ̃ ˈblɒ̃/

hate not to love: the opposite of love

hut a little house, often of wood

fire this is red and hot, and it burns

14

'Very well,' I answered.

So he went back across the glacier and I went after him. Soon we were in his little hut. I sat in front of the fire and listened, and the monster began his story.

When you first made me, I couldn't understand a thing. You looked at me with hate in your eyes and ran away. So I quickly left your rooms. I took a coat and some trousers with me. Soon I learnt about the day and night, hot and cold things, feeling hungry and thirsty, and the sun, the sky, and trees.

One day, some poor people left a little fire by the road, and I found it. It was nice and warm, and I sat by it. But when I put my hand in it, I cried because it **hurt** me.

People were afraid of me, I soon understood. They **screamed** and ran from me when I walked into their villages. So I **travelled** by night across open country and stayed away from villages and towns.

hurt to make someone feel bad

scream to give a loud, high cry because you are afraid

travel to go to different places

One cold, winter night, I found a little house in the **forest** with a hut by it. I went into the hut: from there I could see through a **hole** into the house, but nobody could see me. An old man, a young man, and a young woman lived in the house. They were very poor. They were often hungry, but the two young people always gave the old man the biggest dinner. I nearly cried when I saw that.

From these poor people I learnt language. The old man had one name – *father*. The young woman had different names – *daughter*, *sister*, or *Agatha*. And the young man had different names – *son*, *brother*, or *Felix*. I learnt the names for fire, milk, and bread from them, too. I could watch and listen to them happily for hours. 'They're beautiful,' I thought. One day – soon after that – I saw my face in the water of a lake near the house. I hated it because I wasn't beautiful.

When spring arrived, Felix worked in the garden. He brought the first spring flowers when they came and gave them to his sister. But his face was very sad. On Sundays, the family didn't work. The old man played his guitar and his children listened. (I learnt something more about the old man then: he was **blind**, but he could hear very well.)

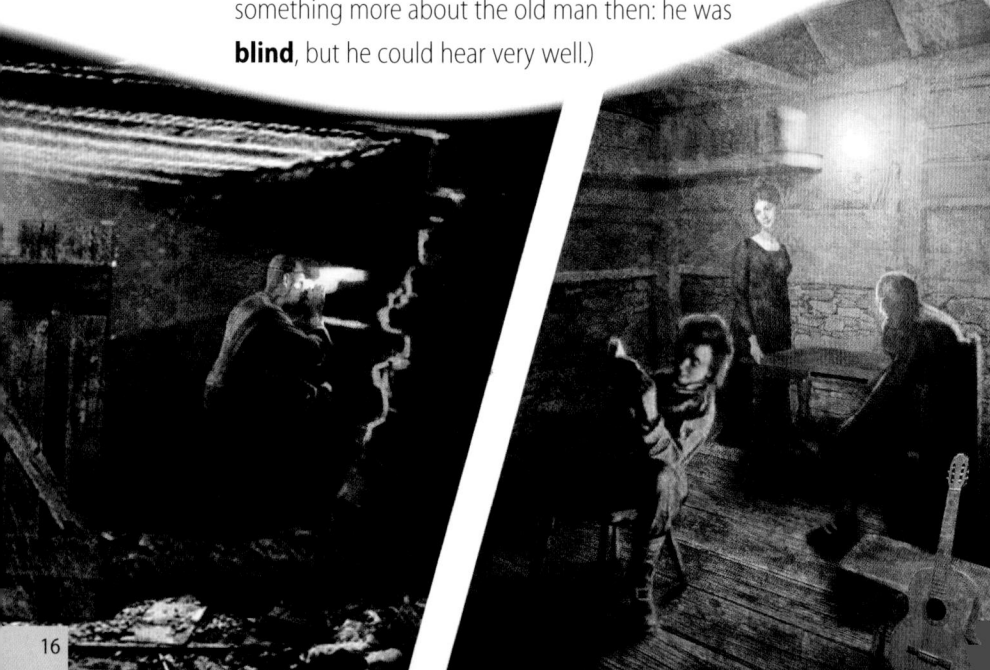

16

One Sunday, when Felix and Agatha listened to their father's guitar, someone arrived at the door. It was a beautiful young woman in a dark dress.

'Safie!' smiled Felix when she came into the house.

Before Felix was sad, but now he was happy. And his sister and father were happy with him.

Soon I understood something. Safie spoke a different language from the old man and his daughter. She needed to learn French. And when Felix taught her, I learnt with her.

I learnt about Safie's story, too. She was the daughter of a Turkish man and an Arab woman. Her mother was dead, and the French **government** put her father in prison for nothing. But the old man – Monsieur De Lacey – was a rich friend of the family. With his son Felix's help, Safie's father got out of prison and left France. Felix met Safie then – before she went away to school in Italy – and began to love her. But when her father was back in Turkey, the French government heard of it. They angrily took all the De Laceys' money and came after them. So the family quickly left for Germany. Poor Safie looked for them in Germany for months before, in the end, she found them.

government
the people who decide what happens in a country

READING CHECK

Correct the mistakes in these sentences.

a ~~Henry Clerval~~ The monster meets Victor in the mountains near Chamonix.

b It wants to write the story of its life.

c Victor goes with the monster to a little mountain hotel.

d The monster begins its story and Victor laughs.

e It took a hat and some trousers when it left Victor's rooms.

f Villagers were happy when they saw it, so it travelled at night.

g One warm night, it found a house in the forest.

h The house belonged to the Frankenstein family.

i The monster watched and spoke to the family.

j Felix was very angry when Safie arrived.

k The monster learned German with Safie.

l Safie's mother went home to Turkey with Felix's help.

m Safie looked for the De Laceys for years after they left France.

WORD WORK

Use the words in the mountain scene to complete the sentences on page 19.

travelling

government

hurt

scream

blind

hates

hut

fire

sad

hole

forest

glacier

18

a Victor feels ......sad......, so he leaves Geneva for the mountains.

b The monster comes across the .... after him.

c Victor .... the monster, but he is afraid of it, too.

d Victor sits near a warm .... and the monster tells its story.

e The monster is .... when Victor runs from it in Ingolstadt.

f The monster doesn't like it when villagers .... noisily at it.

g It begins .... at night because everyone is afraid of it.

h It arrives at the De Laceys' house in a .... in Germany.

i The monster goes into a little .... by the house.

j It watches the family through a little ....

k Monsieur De Lacey is an old, ... man.

l The French .... took all the De Laceys' money.

GUESS WHAT

What happens in the next chapter? Tick five boxes.

The monster …

a ☐ finds one of Victor's books and reads it.

b ☐ writes an angry letter to Victor.

c ☐ speaks to old Monsieur De Lacey.

d ☐ kills all the De Laceys and Safie.

e ☐ walks slowly away through the forest.

f ☐ kills a young girl in a river.

g ☐ travels to Geneva and looks for Victor's home.

h ☐ tells Victor about meeting and killing William.

i ☐ asks Victor for a monster wife.

j ☐ stays with Victor when he leaves the hut.

CHAPTER 4
FEELING ALONE

Not long after that, I went hungrily out into the forest one day. I found a bag with three books in it under a tree. Over time I learnt to read from these books.

When I first arrived at the De Laceys' hut, I found something in one of my coat pockets. This coat, you remember, came from your rooms in Ingolstadt. It was your **journal**. Now I could read, so I took it out and read it. How did my life begin? That journal told me. You, Victor Frankenstein, were my maker. You made me from dead body parts. I felt ill when I read that. I couldn't forget the hate in your eyes when you first looked at me. And the villagers were afraid of me and ran away, too. I hated being **alone**.

Soon after that, I decided to speak to the De Laceys. 'Perhaps they can be my friends,' I thought. I decided to speak to the old, blind father first. 'He can't see my **terrible** face and body. So when we talk, he can listen to a man, not see a monster.'

Some days later, Felix, Safie, and Agatha went out for a walk. They left old Monsieur De Lacey at home. I decided to speak to him then.

When I arrived at his front door, he heard me.

'Who's that?' he called. 'Come in.'

I went in. 'I'm a traveller,' I said, 'and I'd like to sit by your fire.'

'Then sit,' said the old man. 'Are you hungry? My children are out, and I'm blind. But do you want to eat?'

'No, thank you,' I answered. I sat down next to him.

'Are you French?' he asked.

'No, but I learnt to speak from a French family. It's my only language.'

'I see,' said the old man. 'And where are you travelling now?'

'I'm going to visit some friends. I need their help. I'm all alone in life. But I'm afraid ...'

journal a book where you write about what happens every day

alone with nobody

terrible making people afraid; very bad

20

'Of what?' he asked.

'Perhaps they aren't going to help me when they see me.'

'Why? A man's friends must help him when he needs it.'

'But perhaps in their eyes I'm a monster.'

'How can they think that? I must speak to them. Where do they live?'

'Near here,' I answered.

Suddenly I heard Safie, Felix, and Agatha at the door.

I quickly took the old man's hand and said, 'You're my friends: you and Felix and Agatha. Speak to your children. I'm a good man, not a monster – please tell them!'

'What? Who are you?' cried the old man.

Just then, Felix, Safie, and Agatha came in and saw me.

Agatha screamed, Safie ran away, and Felix began hitting me. 'You monster! Leave my father alone,' he cried.

With a terrible cry, I ran into the forest.

'I hate **humans**,' I thought darkly. 'But most of all I hate my maker, Victor Frankenstein.'

I went back to the De Laceys' house for my things later. They left the next morning and never came back. I decided to travel to the Frankenstein family's home in Geneva.

When I was on the Geneva road, I saw a young girl by a river in the forest. She suddenly **fell** in. I went in the river after her, and took her in my arms. Then I carried her out of the water and put her down near the river. She couldn't open her eyes, but she was alive!

Just then, a young man arrived. He saw me with the girl.

'You monster! Take your hands off her!' he cried. Then he took the girl in his arms and ran away with her.

When I went after them, the young man **attacked** me with a **gun**. Angrily, I ran away. I arrived near Lake Geneva that evening.

There, at Plainpalais, I met a young boy. He was not afraid of me. 'Do you know Alphonse Frankenstein's house in Geneva?' I asked him.

'Yes,' he answered. 'Alphonse Frankenstein's my father.'

I was suddenly very angry. I took the boy in my hands and **strangled** him. He wore a locket, I saw. I took this from his dead body. Then I went and quickly put it in a young woman's coat pocket. She sat and half slept under a tree not far away.

human a person, not a monster

fall (*past* **fell**) to go down suddenly

attack to start fighting someone; when you start fighting someone

gun a person can fight with this

strangle to kill someone by putting your hands on their neck, stopping them breathing

female being a woman

I could listen no more. 'So you killed my young brother William, and you put the locket in Justine Moritz's pocket,' I said. 'But why?'

'I hate humans. I want to hurt them all – and you more than any man alive,' he answered.

'You're a monster!' I cried.

'Am I? You made me and then left me. Humans are afraid of me. I have no friends. I need a wife – a **female** monster.

With a wife I can be happy. I can take her far away, and you and your family can be free of me. Make a wife for me, Victor Frankenstein.'

'All right,' I **promised**.

promise to say now that you can do something later; when you say that you can do something later

'Good,' said the monster. 'I'm going to watch your work from far away and wait. Then, when my wife's ready, I'm going to come for her.'

With that, he left the hut and ran away across the glacier.

I arrived back at the village of Chamonix that night. The next day I travelled to Geneva. I needed to see my family.

READING CHECK

Match the two parts of the sentences.

a The monster finds some books in [8]
b It finds Victor's journal in ☐
c One afternoon, it goes to ☐
d It goes and sits in a chair by ☐
e Felix, Agatha, and Safie are walking in ☐
f Suddenly, the three of them arrive at ☐
g The monster runs away and comes to ☐
h The young girl falls down into ☐
i A young man takes the girl from ☐
j The monster meets William in ☐
k It puts William's locket in ☐

1 a river with a young girl by it.
2 its coat pocket and learns about its maker.
3 Justine Moritz's pocket, when she is sleeping.
4 Plainpalais and kills him there.
5 the De Laceys' front door and visits the house.
6 the door, see the monster, and are afraid.
7 the fire and speaks to Monsieur De Lacey.
8 the forest and learns to read with them.
9 the forest for some time that afternoon.
10 the monster, and it runs away to Geneva.
11 the water, but the monster takes her out.

WORD WORK

1 Find nine more words from Chapter 4 in the wordsquare.

P	R	O	M	I	S	E	S	K	C
J	A	L	O	N	E	E	O	D	K
O	T	B	R	F	I	K	L	F	H
U	T	E	R	R	I	B	L	E	U
R	A	F	A	L	L	S	G	M	M
N	C	J	E	K	G	U	W	A	A
A	K	A	C	L	U	L	R	L	N
L	S	T	R	A	N	G	L	E	S

2 Use the words in the wordsquare on page 24 to complete the sentences.

a The monster reads Victor's ...journal....

b It doesn't like having no friends and being ....

c It has a .... face and body, and it knows this.

d It hates all .... – but most of all it hates Victor.

e It goes and helps when a young girl .... into a river.

f A young man is afraid for the girl and .... the monster.

g The monster runs away from the young man and his ....

h The monster .... William Frankenstein with its big hands.

i The monster asks Victor for a .... creature to be its wife.

j Victor .... to make a second monster.

GUESS WHAT

Alphonse

The monster

Henry

**What happens in the next chapter? Complete each sentence with a name.
You can use some names more than once.**

a .... talks to Victor about his love for Elizabeth.

b .... visits London with Victor.

c .... visits Victor in the far north of Scotland.

d .... is angry when Victor stops work suddenly.

e .... writes a letter to Victor.

f .... leaves Ireland quickly in a little boat.

g .... dies in Ireland one night.

CHAPTER 5

TO ENGLAND, SCOTLAND, AND IRELAND

I was **worried** on the road to Geneva.

'Now I must make a second monster!' I thought.

When I arrived home, my father saw my worried face.

'What's the matter?' he asked.

'Nothing, Father,' I answered.

'Victor, please understand. Your mother – before she died – **dreamt** of a **wedding** between you and Elizabeth. I too have this dream. But perhaps you don't want to marry her. Perhaps in your eyes she's nothing more than a sister to you. Am I right? Do you feel that? Then tell me, and let's forget this dream.'

'No, Father, I want to marry Elizabeth,' I answered. 'But I must do something important before our wedding.'

'What's that?' asked my father.

'I'd like to visit England,' I said. I couldn't tell him about the monster and my terrible promise to him. But I wanted to make the female monster in a country far away from my family in Switzerland.

'All right. Then go,' said my father. 'But please take a friend with you. What about Henry Clerval?'

So in the end, Henry came with me. We travelled through Germany to Holland, and then went across the sea by ship to England. We stayed in London for some weeks. Henry visited all the famous buildings. I met and talked with a number of famous English men of science. Soon I was ready for the **creation** of a second monster.

After some time, a letter arrived for us from a Scottish

worried not happy about something and thinking about it a lot

dream (*past* **dreamt**) to think about something nice that you would like to happen; something that you would like to happen

wedding the day when two people marry

creation when you make something; something that you make

friend. He asked us to his house in Perth. So Henry and I left England and travelled up to Scotland. But I left Henry with our friend in Perth and went further north alone – to one of the Scottish **islands**. I took a little house there, and began to work on the creation of a new, female monster from dead body parts.

I worked day and night on this second creature, but I was very worried.

'Is my first monster going to be happy with her?' I thought one night. 'Or perhaps she's not going to be happy with him. What then? Am I truly going to be free of them? Perhaps in time they're going to have children – a family of terrible monsters! How can I stop that? Oh, why did I promise to do this?'

Then I looked up and saw the creature at the open window. He was here! The monster smiled a dark smile at me, and I felt afraid.

'I'm doing something terrible,' I suddenly thought. I looked down at the female monster's body on the table before me. And there and then I began to **destroy** my creation.

island a country, or part of a country, in the sea

destroy to break every part of something

'Noooo!' cried the monster. 'You cannot break your promise to me!'

'I can and I do,' I answered.

'Why can every man have a wife but I must have nobody? I wanted to find love, and you – you give me hate! But remember this: I can hurt you.'

'I'm not afraid of you,' I cried. 'Your dream of a female monster is over. Nothing can change that. Now go.'

'Be careful,' he said. 'I came after you through Germany, Holland, England, and Scotland. You can never leave me behind. I'm going to be with you on your wedding night.'

And with that, the monster left the island in his boat.

The next day, a letter came for me from Henry.

> *Victor,*
>   *Perth isn't very interesting. Come and meet me soon. Let's travel to Ireland.*
>   *Your friend,*
>   *Henry*

I decided to leave the island the next morning. That night, I carried the parts of the female creature's body to a little boat. I took them out to sea, and I put them quickly into the dark waters. After that, I suddenly felt very tired and closed my eyes.

I slept for many hours in the boat. When I opened my eyes again, my boat was on the open sea. The sun was hot and I was very thirsty.

'Am I going to die here?' I thought worriedly. 'Where am I? Is this the Atlantic?'

land the part of the Earth that is not sea; country

But some time later, my boat came near to **land**, and

28

soon I arrived at a little town by the sea.

'There he is!' some of the people from the town cried when I got out of my boat. 'That's the killer!'

'Is this England?' I asked.

'No, Ireland!'

They took me at once to Mr Kirwin, the town judge.

'What's the matter?' I asked him.

'Last night,' Mr Kirwin said, 'a man with a little boat strangled somebody down by the sea. He left the body here, and now you come here in your little boat. So are you the strangler? For many of the people in town, you are. But let's see. Come and look at the dead man.'

I went with him into the next room. The dead body of my good friend Henry Clerval was there on the table!

'Nooo!' I cried. 'He did this! The monster!'

I closed my eyes and fell down suddenly. And I was very ill with a fever for the next two months. Slowly I began to feel better. When I opened my eyes, I was in a prison bed. Mr Kirwin stood by me.

'Ah, you're back with us! That's good because you have a visitor,' he said.

'It's the monster!' I thought. 'He's here because he wants to laugh about Clerval's death!'

'I can't see him!' I cried.

READING CHECK

Correct twelve more mistakes in the story.

> *Geneva*
> Victor goes home to ~~Ingolstadt~~ worriedly. His father speaks to him about his
>
> dead sister's dream – of a wedding between Henry and Elizabeth. Victor wants
>
> to marry Elizabeth, but before the wedding he must visit America! His father
>
> says 'yes' to this, so Victor leaves with Ernest. They stay in London, then go to
>
> Scotland. Victor visits an Irish island alone. He finishes work on a female creature
>
> there. When the monster arrives, Alphonse destroys the female monster. The
>
> monster is angry and leaves. Ernest puts the female monster's body parts in the
>
> sea. By accident, his boat goes to Holland. People take him to the judge of a little
>
> village. Someone killed a woman by the sea there the night before. Elizabeth is
>
> the killer, the villagers think.

WORD WORK

Find words in the boats to complete the sentences.

a Victor feels ...worried... when he goes home. **werrido**

b Victor's .... is marrying Elizabeth. **merad**

c But he must finish with the monster before the .... **dendiwg**

d Victor is soon ready for the .... of a female monster. **taecoinr**

e Victor begins work on one of the Scottish .... **slidsan**

f In the end, Victor .... the monster's wife. **stodsyer**

g After some time at sea, Victor's boat comes near to .... **daln**

GUESS WHAT

What happens in the last chapter? Tick one picture.

a The monster arrives on the ship and kills Victor.

b Victor makes a big fire and kills the monster in it.

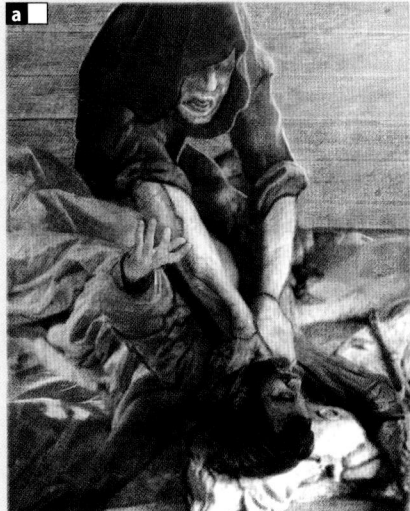

c The monster and Victor die in the cold Arctic sea.

d The monster kills Elizabeth on Victor's wedding night.

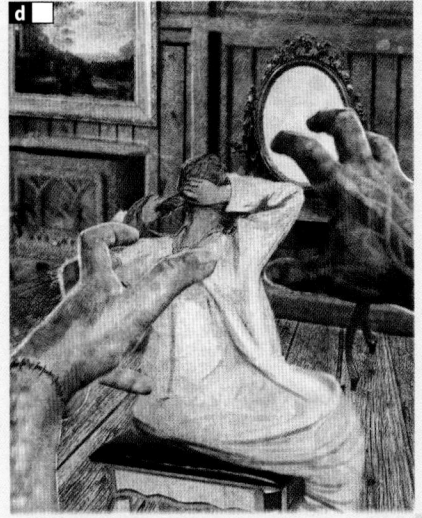

CHAPTER 6
REVENGE AND DEATH

'What's the matter with you?' asked Mr Kirwin. 'Your father's here from Geneva. I found a letter from him in your pocket when you were ill and wrote to him. He came at once, and he wants to see you.'

'Oh, I see!' I answered. 'Of course you can bring Father in.'

My father came in, and we talked.

'Are you alive and well then – and Elizabeth and Ernest, too?'

'Yes, everyone at home is alive and well,' he answered. 'But it's sad news about Clerval!'

'Yes. My poor friend. I killed him, you know, Father. Him and Justine and William – I killed them all.'

'Never say that, Victor. You're ill and you've got a fever. You were on a Scottish island when Clerval died. You didn't kill him.'

My father stayed with me for three months, and I slowly felt better. When I was well again, I went before the judge. He listened carefully to the lawyers' questions and everybody's answers. Then he spoke.

'This man did not kill Henry Clerval,' he said. And so I came out of prison a free man.

Soon after that, my father and I went by ship to France. From there we travelled to Geneva.

'Forget Clerval's sad death, Victor,' said my father. 'And marry Elizabeth.'

Back in Geneva, Elizabeth and I began making **plans** for our wedding. But what did the monster say to me on the Scottish island? 'I'm going to be with you on your wedding night.' I could not forget that.

'Perhaps he wants to attack me and kill me on that night,' I thought. So I began carrying a gun with me in my coat pocket at all times. I wanted to be ready when the monster attacked me. I didn't understand then his terrible plans for me – and for my family.

I told Elizabeth, 'Cousin, there's a terrible **secret** in my life. I can't speak of it now. But I can tell you all about it after we marry.' She looked worried, but did not ask me more about it.

On the day of the wedding, my father was very happy. Elizabeth was quiet and looked sadly beautiful. And I, for a time, forgot to feel afraid.

After the wedding in Geneva, we planned to go and stay at an **inn** in Evian. We took a boat across the lake, and arrived at the inn at eight o'clock in the evening.

Just then, the weather changed and there was a sudden storm over our heads. I felt worried and I put my hand on the gun in my coat pocket.

'What are you afraid of, husband?' asked Elizabeth.

'Once this terrible night is past, I can be free, my love,' I answered her.

'But my wife cannot see the monster's attack on me,' I thought. So I told her, 'Please go upstairs to bed, Elizabeth.

plan when you get something ready to do later; to get something ready to do later

secret something that you don't tell to everybody

inn an old name for a hotel where people can eat, drink, and stay

I can't sleep now. Later perhaps I can come to you.'

She went up to our room. I stayed downstairs and walked up and down with the gun in my hand. But I saw nothing of the monster, and began to feel happier.

Then, suddenly, I heard a woman's screams from upstairs. 'Elizabeth!' I cried. I ran up to our room and quickly opened the door. My wife was there, dead, on the bed. Her long hair was half over her white face, and the window was open to the cold, dark night. 'Her killer left through that window!' I cried. Then I fell down at the end of the bed, and everything went black.

When I opened my eyes, lots of people from the inn were by the bed. I looked over to the window and saw the face of the monster there. He looked across at my dead wife. Then he looked back at me and gave a terrible smile. I got up at once and ran to the window with my gun in my hand. But the creature ran quickly away from the inn and across the snow down to the lake. Some of the men from the inn and I ran after him, but we could not catch him.

They brought me back, tired, to the inn. I slept on a bed there for some time. Then I got up. I was worried for the lives of my father and my brother Ernest.

'I must go back to Geneva tonight!' I cried.

So I left Evian and travelled back to my father's house.

My father and Ernest were alive and well when I arrived. But when I told my father about Elizabeth's sudden death, he took it very badly. The sad and terrible news destroyed him. He went to bed with a fever that night, and he died in my arms three days later.

I went mad after that, and they put me in a hospital for mad people for many weeks. When I was better, my brother Ernest came for me, and I was a free man once more. But I was very angry with the monster. I wanted **revenge** for the deaths of William, Justine, Henry, Elizabeth, and my father. I went to a Geneva lawyer, but he could do nothing for me. So I decided to go after the monster and to destroy him before he could hurt me any more. I left Geneva, hungry for news of the creature. I went after him to Russia, and north to the Arctic. Then I arrived at your ship, Robert Walton. And you took me half-dead from my **sled** and brought me here. Thank you for that. And thank you for listening to my story.

revenge when you do something bad to someone after they do something bad to you

sled a kind of car on skis that dogs pull

Robert Walton, the English man of science, looked sadly across at the poor man on the bed. He felt very sorry for Victor Frankenstein, with his white face and his dark, mad eyes.

'What a terrible story! But is it all true?' he thought.

'I'm going to die soon, I feel it,' Frankenstein said. 'So please promise me one thing, my friend.'

'All right. But what?' asked Walton.

'After I'm dead, you must go after the monster and you must take revenge on him for me. Promise me this one thing, and I can die a happy man.'

'Very well. I promise,' said Walton.

Frankenstein died the next morning.

That afternoon, Walton's men spoke to him.

'Let's leave this land of snow and cold seas, and go back home to England when we can.'

Walton listened to them and decided to take his ship south when the sea-ice broke. 'Science isn't everything,' he thought. 'Family and friends are important, too. And I'd like to see my sister Margaret again soon.'

That afternoon, Walton heard a noise in the next room – the room with Frankenstein's dead body in it. 'Is someone crying there?' he thought.

He quickly opened the door and went into the room. Frankenstein's monster stood by the bed, and terrible cries came from his open mouth.

'What are you doing here?' asked Walton angrily.

'I'm crying for my dead maker,' the monster answered.

'How can you say that after everything that you did to him?' cried Walton. 'You destroyed his life!'

'I know. And I'm sorry for it now,' the monster said. 'I wasn't born a killer. I hated strangling Clerval. But then, back in Switzerland, I heard about Victor's wedding plans and I felt very angry. He destroyed the female monster before my eyes on that Scottish island. How could he marry when I was without a wife? I killed Elizabeth in revenge, and I thought nothing of it. But now I can kill no more.'

The monster looked down sadly at Frankenstein's dead body on the bed before him.

'I'm going to travel north now on my sled,' he said. 'And when I come to the coldest part of this cold land, I'm going to make a big fire and finish my sad life in it. Goodbye.'

And with that, the monster quickly left the room through the open window. And his dog-sled soon took him far away across the snow and ice.

READING CHECK

Put these sentences in the correct order. Number them 1–15.

a ☐ When Victor is well again, he goes before the judge.

b ☐ Elizabeth goes to bed, but Victor stays downstairs with a gun.

c ☐ Alphonse Frankenstein visits his son in prison in Ireland.

d ☐ Victor and his father go back to Geneva.

e ☐ Victor hears screams upstairs and finds Elizabeth dead.

f ☐ Walton promises revenge on the monster, and Victor dies.

g ☐ Victor sees the monster at the window, but it runs away.

h ☐ Victor goes back worriedly to his father and Ernest in Geneva.

i ☐ Victor's father dies days after he hears the news about Elizabeth.

j ☐ The monster leaves over the Arctic snow and plans to die in a fire.

k ☐ The monster comes and cries over Victor's dead body.

l ☐ Walton promises to leave for England when the sea-ice breaks.

m ☐ Victor goes north after the monster and arrives at Walton's ship.

n ☐ The judge says Victor is a free man.

o ☐ Victor marries Elizabeth and they go to an inn in Evian.

ACTIVITIES

WORD WORK

Complete the sentences with the words in the ship.

secret

planning

plans

inn

sled

revenge

a In Geneva, Victor and Elizabeth make lots of wonderful ..... plans ..... for their wedding.

b They decide to stay the night at an old .... in Evian.

c They are .... to visit the town and drink some Evian water there the next day.

d Victor promises to tell his wife Elizabeth all about his terrible .... once their wedding night is past.

e When Elizabeth dies, Victor wants to have .... on the monster, and so he goes after it to Russia.

f He travels far across the Arctic snow on a dog-................. .

GUESS WHAT

What happens after the story finishes? Choose from these ideas or add your own.

a ☐ Ernest goes to Ingolstadt University and learns languages there.

b ☐ Henry Clerval's father closes his shop and dies soon after.

c ☐ Robert Walton meets his sister Margaret in England.

d ☐ Walton tells Margaret all about Victor Frankenstein.

e ☐ Margaret laughs at Walton's story and calls him 'mad'.

f ☐ Walton writes a book about Victor Frankenstein.

g ☐ Walton is soon famous and never leaves England again.

h ☐ A friend of Walton's travels to the Arctic.

i ☐ He finds Victor's journal in the dead monster's coat pocket.

j ☐ He reads the journal and makes a new, more terrible monster.

k ☐ ....

l ☐ ....

Project A *A character acrostic poem*

In an acrostic poem, the first letters of the lines spell
a name when you read them down the page.

1 **Complete the acrostic poems about Victor Frankenstein with the words or names in the boxes.**

> clever   countries   Geneva   monster   secret   years

V ery .... young man,
I ngolstadt .... -maker,
C omes from .... ,
T ravels to different .... ,
O lder than his .... ,
R ich, but with a terrible ....

> alchemists   brother   England   German
> husband   Justine   life   mother
> revenge   son   William   young

F eels happy when he's .... ,
R eads about old .... ,
A lphonse's oldest .... ,
N ice to his .... when she's ill,
K nows French and .... ,
E rnest's older ....
N o help to .... in prison,
S ad at little .... 's death.
T akes Henry to .... ,
E lizabeth's .... for a day,
I n the end, destroys his ....
N ever takes .... !

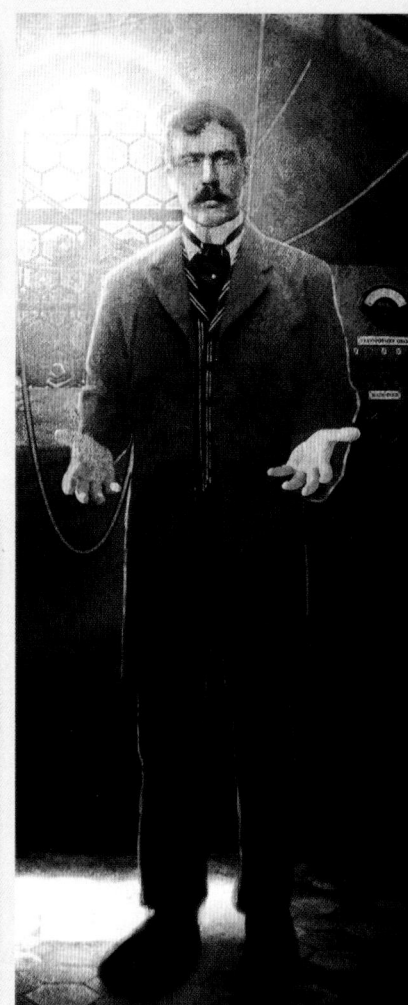

2 Now choose a different character from the story and write an acrostic poem about them. Use a dictionary to help you.

Elizabeth Lavenza

Henry Clerval

Monsieur De Lacey

The Monster

Justine Moritz

Alphonse Frankenstein

Judge Kirwin

3 When everybody's poems are ready, put them up on the classroom wall. Then visit your 'acrostic poem exhibition'.

41

Project B — *A famous horror story*

1 Read the text about *Frankenstein* and complete the table below. Use a dictionary to help you.

Mary Shelley

Frankenstein is a world famous horror story. The English writer Mary Shelley wrote it between 1816 and 1817. The book first came out in 1818, in London. *Frankenstein* tells the story of a young scientist – Victor Frankenstein – and his secret creation, the monster – with its terribly scarred body. At first, Victor makes the monster from parts of dead bodies. Then he brings it alive. In the end, the monster kills Victor's brother, best friend, and wife, and destroys the young scientist's life. The story has a message: new ideas in science can be dangerous.

There are many films of the story, including the 1994 film *Mary Shelley's Frankenstein* – with Robert de Niro playing the monster, and the 1974 comedy film *Young Frankenstein* – with Gene Wilder playing Victor Frankenstein's American grandson, Frederick.

What is the name of the story?	
Who wrote it and when?	
When and where did the book first come out?	
Who are the main characters in the story?	
What happens in the story?	
What is the message of the story?	
What films are there of the story? When did they come out? Who are the actors?	

PROJECTS

2 Use the notes in the table to complete the text about *The Phantom of the Opera* on page 44.

Gaston Leroux

The Phantom of the Opera

What is the name of the story?	The Phantom of the Opera
Who wrote it and when?	French writer Gaston Leroux between 1909 and 1910
When and where did the book first come out?	In 1919, in Paris
Who are the main characters in the story?	A young singer – Christine Daaé and her secret singing teacher Erik (The Phantom), with his terribly scarred face.
What happens in the story?	- The Phantom teaches Christine to sing beautifully. - He takes her prisoner in the Paris Opera House. - She escapes and marries her friend and lover Raoul.
What is the message of the story?	Love is stronger than hate.
What films are there of the story? When did they come out? Who are the actors?	2004 musical The Phantom of the Opera – Gerard Butler playing the Phantom; 1974 sci-fi musical Phantom of the Paradise – William Finley playing a rock star Phantom.

43

The Phantom of the Opera is a world famous horror story. The .... writer .... wrote it between .... and .... The book first came out in .... , in .... *The Phantom of the Opera* tells the story of a young .... – .... – and her secret .... , the .... , with his terribly scarred .... The .... teaches .... to sing .... Then he takes her .... in the .... In the end, she .... and .... her .... and .... , ... The story has a message: .... is .... than ....

There are many films of the story, including the .... film *The Phantom of the Opera* – with .... playing the .... , and the .... - .... *Phantom of the* .... – with .... playing a ....

3 **Choose another famous horror story. Find out information about it on the Internet. Write a short text about it.**

Dr Jekyll and Mr Hyde

The Mummy

The Picture of Dorian Gray

GRAMMAR

GRAMMAR CHECK

Past Simple Yes/No questions and short answers

We use was/were, or the auxiliary verbs did and could + infinitive without *to* in Yes/No questions in the Past Simple.

Was Elizabeth the daughter of a French woman and Milanese man?

Did she have yellow hair and blue eyes?

In the short answer, we repeat the subject and re-use the auxiliary verb or was/were.

No, she wasn't.

Yes, she did.

1 Write answers for the questions. Use the short answers in the box.

> No, they didn't.   No, they weren't.   Yes, she could.
> No, she didn't.   Yes, she did.   Yes, they did.
> No, she wasn't.   ~~Yes, they were.~~   Yes, she was.

a Were the family by Lake Como poor? …Yes, they were.…………

b Did they have six children? …………………………………

c Was Victor's mother interested in Elizabeth? …………………………………

d Did Elizabeth make a lot of noise when she was young? …………………………………

e Did her mother die when she was born? …………………………………

f Were things easy for the poor family by the lake? …………………………………

g Was Elizabeth older than Victor? …………………………………

h Did the Frankensteins take Elizabeth to Geneva? …………………………………

i Could Elizabeth speak Italian and French? …………………………………

2 Write short answers for these questions about Victor.

a Was Victor born in Naples? ……Yes, he was.…………

b Was he the Frankensteins' only son? …………………………………

c Did he play with Elizabeth when he was a boy? …………………………………

d Did he live in Geneva before Ernest was born? …………………………………

e Was he interested in science at fifteen? …………………………………

f Could he speak French and German? …………………………………

GRAMMAR

GRAMMAR CHECK

Verb + infinitive or –*ing* form of verb

Some verbs, like *begin, decide, forget, learn, need, remember,* and *want* are followed by *to* + infinitive.

I wanted to go home to Geneva.

Some verbs, like *begin, go, finish, like, love,* and *stop* are followed by the –ing form of the verb.

William and Ernest went walking in the country.

There is no difference in meaning between *begin* + –*ing* form of the verb / *to* + infinitive.

Lawyers began questioning / to question Justine.

3 **Choose the correct word or words to complete the sentences.**

a Victor stopped (*learning*) / *to learn* science.

b He began *feeling* / *feel* ill when people talked about it.

c He remembered *thank* / *to thank* his teachers.

d He didn't want *to leave* / *leaving* Ingolstadt in the winter.

e Victor went *walk* / *walking* in the mountains with Henry.

f He liked *see* / *seeing* the blue skies over his head.

g He loved *looking* / *look* at the beautiful spring flowers.

h Victor forgot to *feel* / *feeling* afraid up in the mountains.

i He read the letter and decided *to go* / *going* home at once.

j He needed *being* / *to be* with his father just then.

4 **Complete the sentences. Use the infinitive or –*ing* form of the verbs in brackets.**

a Justine needed ...*to answer*......... (answer) the lawyers' questions carefully.

b She didn't want .... (say) the wrong thing.

c She began .... (cry) when Elizabeth and Victor arrived.

d She loved .... (talk) to the two of them.

e Justine didn't like .... (think) about poor William's death.

f She stopped .... (say) 'no' when the priest called her a killer.

g She decided .... (answer) 'yes' because she felt tired.

GRAMMAR CHECK

Linkers: *so* and *because*

We use so to link two sentences when the second sentence explains a result.

The mountains were beautiful so Victor felt very happy. (= result of first part of sentence)

We use because to link two sentences when the second sentence explains a reason.

Victor felt sad the next day because the weather was bad. (= reason for first part of sentence)

5 Match a–i with 1–9. Write complete sentences using *so* or *because*.

a Victor felt terrible …

Victor felt terrible because William and Justine were dead.

b He needed to do something different …

....

c He went to Chamonix on his horse …

....

d He wanted to go up the mountain …

....

e He felt ill …

....

f He went and heard the monster's story …

....

g The monster's hut had a fire in it …

....

h Villagers were afraid of the monster …

....

i The monster wanted a wife …

....

1 he got up early.

2 he left for the mountains.

3 he saw the monster on the glacier.

4 it felt very alone.

5 it spoke of killing more of Victor's family.

6 it was warm.

7 it wasn't very near.

8 they screamed.

9 William and Justine were dead.

GRAMMAR CHECK

Adverbs of manner

We use adverbs of manner to talk about how we do things.

The monster went hungrily out into the forest.

The girl suddenly fell into the river.

We make adverbs from adjectives by adding –ly.

sudden – suddenly

For adjectives that end in –y, we change y to –ily.

hungry – hungrily

6 Write the adverbs of these adjectives.

   a slow . . . . . *slowly* . . . .   **e** wrong . . . .

   b quick . . . .   **f** bad . . . .

   c blind . . . .   **g** angry . . . .

   d happy . . . .   **h** careful . . . .

7 Complete each sentences using an adverb from Activity 6.

   a The monster . . . . . *slowly* . . . . learnt to read. This took many weeks.

   b The monster hated being alone. It needed friends . . . .

   c With smiles on their faces, they went out . . . . for a walk.

   d The old man saw nothing. He sat
      . . . . by the fire.

   e He listened . . . . to the
      monster and asked many questions.

   f 'A monster's attacking that girl!' the
      young man thought, ...

   g 'Grrr!' the monster cried
      . . . ., and then it
      strangled William.

   h It . . . . put the locket in her
      pocket. This took no time at all.

GRAMMAR CHECK

Going to future: affirmative, negative, and questions

We make the *going to* future with subject + the verb *be* (*not*) + *going to* + infinitive.
We use the *going to* future for plans, intentions, and predictions with evidence now.

I'm going to make the female monster far from home. (plan)

She's not going to be happy with him. (prediction)

I'm not going to do this! (intention)

In *going to* questions, the order is the verb *be* (*not*) + subject + *going to* + infinitive.

Are you going to break your promise?

8 **Put the words in order and write affirmative or negative *going to* sentences.
Use contractions where possible.**

a monster / going / is / to / mad / go / the / .

   The monster's going to go mad.

b wife / a / not / have / it / to / going / is / .

   ....

c not / are / move / to / going / South America / they / to / .

   ....

d is / going / come back / to / his / on / night /wedding / the monster /.

   ....

e going / to / more / people / are / die /.

   ....

9 **Imagine the female monster is in the sea. Write *going to* questions with
these words.**

a lightning / hit / the sea / ?

   Is lightning going to hit the sea?

b it / travel / through / the water / ?

   ....

c the female monster / come / alive / ?

   ....

d first monster / meet / her / ?

   ....

GRAMMAR CHECK

Modal auxiliary verbs: can, can't, and must

We use can + infinitive without *to* to describe things that we are able to do or that are possible.

'Of course you can bring Father in,' I told Mr Kirwin.

We use can't + infinitive without *to* to describe things that we are not able to do or that are not possible.

'I can't speak of this terrible secret now,' I told my wife.

We use must + infinitive without *to* to describe things that we have to do or that are an obligation.

'I must go back to Geneva tonight!' I cried.

10 **Choose the best verb to complete each sentence.**

a 'You ⟨must⟩/ can't never say that. You didn't kill them!' my father told me.

b 'You didn't kill Henry Clerval. So you *can / can't* go free,' said Judge Kirwin.

c 'Listen to me, Victor: you *must / can* forget your friend Clerval's sad death,' my father began.

d 'And you *must / can't* marry Elizabeth when we arrive home,' he finished.

e 'We *must / can't* go out into the inn garden. It's raining,' said Elizabeth.

f 'Perhaps I *can / must* kill the monster with this gun,' I thought.

g 'I *can't / can* tell you my terrible secret after we marry, but not now,' I said to Elizabeth.

h 'I *can / can't* sleep tonight because I'm very worried,' I told my wife.

i 'You *must / can't* go up to bed now. You're tired!' I said to Elizabeth.

j 'I *can't / can* forget the monster's promise to come back on my wedding night,' I thought.

k 'There's the monster. Quickly! We *can't / must* stop him! Let's go after him!' I cried.

l 'You *can / can't* come out of hospital now. You're not mad any more,' said Ernest.

GRAMMAR CHECK

Present Simple information questions

We use question words – how, who, what, why, where, and when – in information questions. We answer these questions with information. With the verb *be*, the word order is question word + *be* + subject.

Who is Robert Walton? Victor's last friend.

With other verbs, we put an auxiliary verb before the subject.

How does Walton look at Victor? Sadly.

After the auxiliary verb do/does + subject, we use infinitive without *to*.

What do Walton and Victor talk about? Victor's life.

1 Complete each question about Robert Walton with a word in the box. Match the answers below with the questions.

> How ~~What~~ What What When Where Which Which Who Why

a ......What...... is the name of Robert Walton's sister? 3

b ....country does Walton come from?

c ....is his ship at the moment?

d ....does Walton promise Victor?

e ....does he suddenly decide to leave the Arctic?

f ....is he going to take his ship south?

g ....three things in life are important for Walton?

h ....is on the bed in the room next to Walton's?

i ....does Walton hear in that room after Victor dies?

j ....does Walton speak when he talks to the monster?

1 Britain.

2 Angrily.

3 Margaret.

4 Victor Frankenstein.

5 In the cold Arctic ice.

6 When the sea-ice breaks.

7 The monster's terrible cries.

8 Science, family, and friends.

9 Because his men ask him to.

10 To take revenge on the monster.

DOMINOES Your Choice

Read *Dominoes* for pleasure, or to develop language skills. It's your choice.

Each *Domino* reader includes:
- a good story to enjoy
- integrated activities to develop reading skills and increase vocabulary
- task-based projects – perfect for CEFR portfolios
- contextualized grammar activities

Each *Domino* pack contains a reader, and an excitingly dramatized audio recording of the story

If you liked this *Domino*, read these:

Jake's Parrot
Paul Hearn and Yetis Ozkan

When Jake Stevens goes to work for some months in Ireland, he feels happy. He loves travelling, and talking about his job – making computer games for BananaTech in America. 'Your new game's going to be the best thing at the Irish Computer Games Show!' people at BananaTech Ireland tell him.

But living with a noisy parrot isn't easy, and when Jake asks the most beautiful girl at work out to dinner, she says 'no'.

Then someone steals Jake's game the night before the show. Who – or what – can help him to get it back?

Mystery in Muscat
Julie Till

'How long is she in Oman for?'

'Ten days. And then they want to take her back home.'

'Ah, yes. But she's not going back to London. They're never going to see her again!'

Jamie and Taymour overhear this strange conversation near their homes in Muscat. Two men want to kill an important visitor, it seems. But who is the woman in danger? And what can the boys do to save her?

Can they, their sisters Sarah and Nadine, and their Australian friend Ruth find the answer to the mystery?

	CEFR	Cambridge Exams	IELTS	TOEFL iBT	TOEIC
Level 3	B1	PET	4.0	57-86	550
Level 2	A2–B1	KET-PET	3.0-4.0	–	390
Level 1	A1–A2	YLE Flyers/KET	3.0	–	225
Starter & Quick Starter	A1	YLE Movers	1.0–2.0	–	– –

You can find details and a full list of books and teachers' resources on our website:
www.oup.com/elt/gradedreaders